RECRUITING VOLUNTEERS

A Guide for Non-Profits

Mary Ann Burke
Carl Liljenstolpe

CRISP PUBLICATIONS, INC.
Los Altos, California

RECRUITING VOLUNTEERS
A Guide for Non-Profits

Mary Ann Burke
and Carl Liljenstolpe

CREDITS:
Editor: **Beverly M. Manber Mauber**
Designer: **Carol Harris**
Typesetting: **ExecuStaff**
Cover Design: **Carol Harris**
Artwork: **Ralph Mapson**

Copyright © 1992 Crisp Publications, Inc.
Printed in the United States of America by Bawden Printing Company.

English language Crisp books are distributed worldwide. Our major international distributors include:

CANADA: Reid Publishing, Ltd., Box 69559—109 Thomas St., Oakville, Ontario Canada L6J 7R4. TEL: (416) 842-4428; FAX: (416) 842-9327

AUSTRALIA: Career Builders, P.O. Box 1051, Springwood, Brisbane, Queensland, Australia 4127. TEL: 841-1061, FAX: 841-1580

NEW ZEALAND: Career Builders, P.O. Box 571, Manurewa, Auckland, New Zealand. TEL: 266-5276, FAX: 266-4152

JAPAN: Phoenix Associates Co., Mizuho Bldg. 2-12-2, Kami Osaki, Shinagawa-Ku, Tokyo 141, Japan. TEL: 3-443-7231, FAX: 3-443-7640

Selected Crisp titles are also available in other languages. Contact International Rights Manager Tim Polk at (415) 949-4888 for more information.

Library of Congress Catalog Card Number 91-76308
Burke, Mary Ann and Liljenstolpe, Carl
Recruiting Volunteers
ISBN 1-56052-141-4

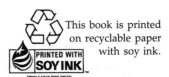

This book is printed on recyclable paper with soy ink.

PREFACE

This book has been developed for two audiences: nonprofit organizations that rely on volunteers to accomplish their missions and goals, and community volunteer organizations (e.g., schools and boosters, sports, civic and hobby groups).

Nonprofit staff support funding is becoming scarce. In response, nonprofit organizations are developing innovative solutions to meet their labor shortage needs.

Recruitment and development of volunteer labor pools has never been stronger; however, if planning is short-sighted, volunteer recruitment and development can undermine an organization's daily operations.

If you are considering using volunteers for the first time, this book will provide a model for developing an effective volunteer program.

If your organization has utilized volunteers for many years, the book will assist you in:

- Reassessing Your Use of Volunteers
- Identifying New Functional Roles For Volunteers
- Considering Innovative Recruitment Strategies
- Designing Comprehensive Volunteer Training
- Creating An Ongoing Volunteer Evaluation

Regardless of your past volunteer experiences, this book will guide you through the process of:

- Determining the Value of Volunteers
- Clarifying Your Organization's Mission
- Identifying the Roles of Each Functional Area
- Utilizing Volunteers Throughout the Organization
- Understanding Volunteer Recruitment Options
- Assigning and Developing Volunteers

It will help you empower volunteers to most effectively meet the needs of your organization.

Kudos to the many volunteers who give of themselves for the betterment of others.

i

ABOUT THIS BOOK

Recruiting Volunteers has a unique "self-paced" format that encourages a reader to become personally involved. Designed to be "read with a pencil," this book contains an abundance of exercises that invite participation.

The objective of *Recruiting Volunteers* is to help individuals and organizations define the value of volunteers, evaluate the roles of volunteers, and develop programs to insure the effective use of volunteers.

Recruiting Volunteers and other self-improvement books listed at the back of the book are valuable in several ways:

Individual Study. Because the book is self-instructional, all that is needed is a quiet place, time and a pencil. Completing all the activities and exercises will provide practical steps for self-improvement.

Workshops and Seminars. This book is ideal as pre-assigned reading prior to a formal training session. With the basics in hand, more time can be spent on concept extensions and advanced applications. This book is also effective when used as a part of a workshop or seminar.

Remote Location Training. Copies can be sent to those not able to attend "home office" training sessions. *Recruiting Volunteers* also makes an excellent "desk reference book."

There are other possibilities that depend on the needs or objectives of the user. You are invited to find uses that will provide benefits for your program.

CONTENTS

INTRODUCTION

As summarized below, *Recruiting Volunteers* takes the reader through the systematic process of defining his or her agency's mission, identifying the organization's roles and responsibilities, evaluating the roles and perceived value of volunteers, and analyzing cost benefits associated with volunteers.

Finally, the reader develops his or her own practical system to recruit, qualify and develop the agency's volunteer staff.

SECTION I—THE VALUE OF VOLUNTEERS

Using a variety of worksheets, you will have the opportunity to evaluate your perception of volunteers and their value in your organization. This information will enable you to assess how to further develop your volunteer program.

SECTION II—YOUR NONPROFIT ORGANIZATION'S STRATEGIC PLAN

Once you assess your organization's mission and identify your agency's goals, you will be able to determine the various roles and responsibilities of volunteers.

SECTION III—DEFINING AND RECRUITING VOLUNTEERS

Completing the work sheets will give you an opportunity to write a job description for a specific volunteer responsibility. After reviewing the various recruitment strategies, you will determine appropriate methods for recruiting volunteers with specific skills.

SECTION IV—VOLUNTEER ASSIGNMENT AND DEVELOPMENT

Volunteers are hard to keep. You will learn how to assess, train and motivate your volunteers.

SECTION

I

The Value
of Volunteers

The Volunteer Challenge

Volunteer organizations have limited understanding of how to effectively use volunteers. Typically, when a volunteer offers time and skills to an agency, the agency does not fully comprehend the volunteer's value.

With appropriate freedom, support, direction and mentorship, the volunteer can become empowered to fulfill an agency's:

- ACTIVITIES
- MISSIONS
- GOALS
- DREAMS
- OBJECTIVES

This section will help you to identify your volunteers' value and use. Based upon this information, you will determine how to further develop your volunteer program.

CHARACTERISTICS OF EFFECTIVE VOLUNTEERS

Effective volunteers possess a variety of talents and capabilities. To nurture appropriate volunteer opportunities, your organization must identify characteristics that are most valuable for your organization's effectiveness.

List the attributes that you have observed in your volunteers, your staff, yourself or others that enhance your organization's effectiveness. Examples include a positive attitude, innovation, a sense of humor, adaptability, and belief in the organization's mission.

_____

_____

_____

_____

_____

_____

_____

Determine the Value of Volunteers

For most nonprofit organizations, staff support funding is becoming more scarce. When considering this, volunteer organizations will usually recruit any volunteer that approaches the agency. Without proper volunteer skill assessment and adequate job function planning, the relationship between the volunteer and the agency can be severely strained.

To best utilize a volunteer's unique skills, interests and commitment to the agency, prepare a cost/benefit analysis for each job function in the organization. This analysis will:

- Determine the monetary value of having a volunteer perform the specific function

- Help you restructure your organization to provide adequate volunteer support and resources

- Identify how to best utilize a volunteer

- Identify the monetary value of a specific volunteer function

A COST/BENEFIT ANALYSIS OF A VOLUNTEER FUNCTION

Answer the following questions for each function currently performed by volunteers. If your agency is not currently using volunteers in a specific function, this analysis will identify the cost saving of having a volunteer perform the function.

STEP 1: What would be the monthly cost to compensate an employee to perform this specific volunteer function?

_____

STEP 2: What would be the cost to train an employee or volunteer to adequately perform the tasks?

_____

STEP 3: How many months will a volunteer commit to perform this specific function?

_____

STEP 4: Multiply the answer to Step 1 by the answer to Step 3. Add this number to the answer to Step 2. This is the total value of the specific volunteer function.

_____

Record the answer to Step 4, the Lifetime Value of a Volunteer, on the Volunteer Value Statement on the next page.

VOLUNTEER VALUE STATEMENT

Volunteer Organization

Volunteer Function

Lifetime Value of a Volunteer

Date

Post this volunteer value statement as a constant reminder of the true worth of this volunteer function in your organization.

POSSIBLE ROLES FOR VOLUNTEERS

Volunteers provide a variety of agency services. Examine the following nonprofit organizational chart to visualize where volunteers can contribute their talents most effectively in your organization:

Volunteer Services Support Structure

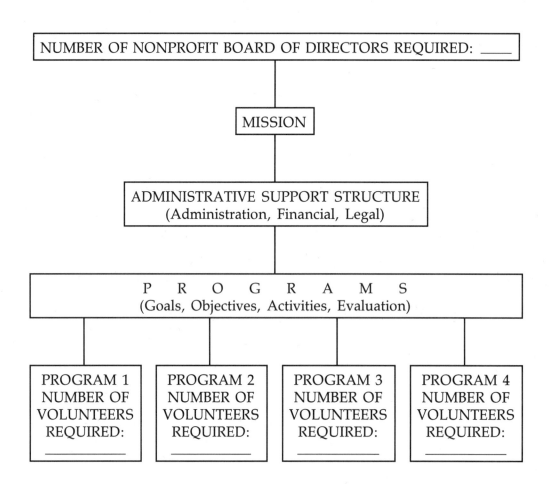

VOLUNTEER USAGE EXAMPLE

Most nonprofit organizations use volunteers to assist with various administrative functions, to support program activities, and to serve as board members. A clear definition of the functional areas within the organizational structure increases potential utilization of volunteers.

The following exercise demonstrates the process to determine how volunteers can be utilized most effectively within an organization:

Program: Human Service Information and Referral

Primary Goals:

- Provide information about appropriate human services to inquiring callers.
- Maintain a telephone log on the number of daily inquiries and the type of requests.
- Summarize the number and type of requests in a monthly report.
- Update the information and referral database as required.

Based on these goals, list four basic support roles that a volunteer could perform:

1. _____

_____

2. _____

_____

3. _____

_____

4. _____

_____

VOLUNTEER USAGE EXAMPLE (continued)

In addition to the basic support roles of an agency function, a volunteer can perform numerous supplementary roles. Using the previous example, list four additional services a volunteer could provide that would enhance the program:

1. _____

_____

2. _____

_____

3. _____

_____

4. _____

_____

Additional information and referral program activities might include:

- Researching communication strategy to determine other communication support services that could be provided to callers.

- Researching other human service information and referral programs offered in similar communities. Compare services.

- Attending human service planning meetings in the community. Share meeting information with appropriate agency staff.

- Serving on a community needs assessment committee or human service task force.

- Identifying the current gaps in human services based upon the information and referral reports.

- Writing public relations articles about human service requests and needs.

WHEN A VOLUNTEER IS GIVEN THE FREEDOM TO CONTRIBUTE SUPPLEMENTARY SUPPORT ACTIVITIES IN OTHER PROJECT AREAS:

- the effectiveness of the entire organization will be enhanced

- the effectiveness of the functional area will expand

- the volunteer contributions to the organization will increase

- the volunteer role within the organization will improve

CREATE A VOLUNTEER SKILLS BANK

Using one of your agency programs that volunteers currently support, answer the following questions:

What is the program's title?

_____

_____

What are the primary program goals?

_____

_____

_____

_____

_____

What roles do the volunteers provide in this program?

_____

_____

_____

_____

_____

What supplementary services could volunteers provide in this program?

_____

_____

_____

_____

_____

How can the supplementary services you listed above benefit other functional areas within your organization?

_____

_____

_____

_____

_____

Identify the skills required to support each volunteer role in the program:

_____

_____

_____

_____

_____

_____

For each volunteer role, identify additional skills required to perform supplementary services:

_____

_____

_____

_____

_____

_____

SKILL IDENTIFICATION

List the skills you have identified as required to fully support the agency program:

_____   _____   _____

_____   _____   _____

_____   _____   _____

_____   _____   _____

_____   _____   _____

In the next few pages, you will examine further the various functional areas within your organization. Through this analysis, you will identify skills required for other functional areas. Once you have listed all skills required for your organization, you can create a volunteer skills bank and effectively assign, coordinate and utilize the unique talents of each of your agency's volunteers.

S E C T I O N

II

Your Nonprofit Organization's Strategic Plan

Assess Your Organization's Mission

Various values, assumptions and beliefs are considered when a nonprofit organization creates its mission statement. Initially, the agency will research and develop an environmental scan on a particular human service need. It will also study various strategies for responding effectively to a human service need.

Once an appropriate strategy is identified, the agency creates a comprehensive long-range plan. Each year the nonprofit organization will examine and update its agency plan, reflecting the changes in the community.

NONPROFIT OVERALL EVALUATION

Answer the following questions about your nonprofit organization. Then ask these questions of others who hear you talk about your organization or have had some contact with your services:

- What stands out most when you think about your agency?

- What one characteristic or adjective best describes your agency?

- What do I think of when I think of my agency?

- What do I elaborate on the most when I talk about my agency?

- What really excites me about my agency?

- What frustrates me the most about my agency?

- Do any of the answers I have listed relate to my organization's values, beliefs, assumptions or mission? If so, how?

- What have I learned about my agency from these questions?

HOW WELL DOES YOUR AGENCY DELIVER?

Consider the benefits and limitations of the listed characteristics as they relate to your agency. Circle the appropriate numerical value for each item.

	Low			High	
1. Type of community in which the agency is located	1	2	3	4	5
2. The location of the agency in the community	1	2	3	4	5
3. Agency atmosphere and furnishings	1	2	3	4	5
4. Office equipment	1	2	3	4	5
5. Facility maintenance	1	2	3	4	5
6. Availability of beverages and food	1	2	3	4	5
7. Employee relations within the agency	1	2	3	4	5
8. Employee relations outside the agency	1	2	3	4	5
9. Employees' availability to clients	1	2	3	4	5
10. Employees' response to clients	1	2	3	4	5
11. Management style within the agency	1	2	3	4	5
12. Management's image outside the agency	1	2	3	4	5
13. Organization's culture	1	2	3	4	5
14. Agency's involvement in the community	1	2	3	4	5
15. Agency's benefit package	1	2	3	4	5
16. Agency's social activities	1	2	3	4	5
17. Agency's program services	1	2	3	4	5
18. Agency's service availability	1	2	3	4	5
19. Agency's service fees	1	2	3	4	5
20. Agency's commitment to follow-through	1	2	3	4	5

	Low			High	
21. Agency's timely delivery of services	1	2	3	4	5
22. Agency's guarantee of service quality	1	2	3	4	5
23. Ease of doing business with the agency	1	2	3	4	5
24. Organization's integrity	1	2	3	4	5
25. Agency's commitment to its mission	1	2	3	4	5

Comments on the three highest scoring characteristics:

_____

_____

_____

Comments on the three lowest scoring characteristics:

_____

_____

_____

Based upon your responses to this survey, discuss how your agency is living its mission in being responsive to the community, its employees and its volunteers:

_____

_____

_____

_____

_____

_____

VISUALIZE YOUR NONPROFIT ORGANIZATION'S FUTURE

Visualizing your organization's future requires the following:

► An optimistic attitude about the future and your agency's response to it

► A permissive and supportive environment that promotes risk-taking, initiative and creativity

► Adaptability and openness to change

► Lack of initial constraints based upon logic or limited resources

► Respectful understanding that a vision may not be clearly, succinctly or completely articulated until further explored.

► Visions can be developed by anyone who has a vested interest in the organization, and the agency's growth is directly correlated to the expansiveness of the visions. Effective visions consider the people involved (i.e. clients, volunteers, employees, the community) and can be articulated most easily when broken into small steps, over a long period of time. Effective visions inspire as they change the world.

Once an organization's vision for the future is identified, the following are essential for successful implementation:

► The vision must be clearly stated.

► Top management must clearly support the vision.

► Top management must promote the vision and encourage full cooperation and support.

► Resources must be allocated, as required.

► The entire organization must embody the vision and share it with the world.

HOW DOES YOUR AGENCY MEASURE UP?

List the characteristics or accomplishments that make your agency unique:

_____

_____

_____

_____

List your agency's current limitations and challenges:

_____

_____

_____

_____

VISUALIZATION EXERCISE

Close your eyes and think about your agency's values, beliefs, assumptions and mission. Let your mind drift. Visualize your agency responding to human needs, without financial restraints or limited resources. Ask yourself the following questions:

1. How can my agency empower the community?

2. What services will my agency provide to meet this empowerment?

3. Who is involved in this empowerment?

4. How are these people empowering each other?

5. Over what time period is this empowerment occurring?

6. What will this system look like one year from now?

7. What changes will occur in the system during the next five, ten and twenty years?

8. What unlimited resources will we need to fulfill this dream?

Open your eyes. In the space below, sketch your vision of your agency's future:

My Vision of My Agency's Future

Do you feel excited, sad or at peace with your vision? What is missing from your vision?

After illustrating your vision, write a summary statement about it:

The future vision of my agency is _____

_____

_____

_____

Identify four main goals to make your vision a reality.

The four main goals to accomplish this vision include:

1. _____

   _____

2. _____

   _____

3. _____

   _____

4. _____

   _____

Share your vision with your agency and develop an implementation plan that will make your dream become a reality. Start living your vision for your agency's future today!

Identify Your Organization's Various Functions

After formulating your agency's vision and workplan for the future, identify functional areas within your organization. List each program area, as well as the major administrative services within your organization.

1. _____
2. _____
3. _____
4. _____
5. _____
6. _____
7. _____
8. _____
9. _____
10. _____
11. _____
12. _____

NEW FUNCTIONAL AREAS

Now, considering your agency's vision and workplan for the future, review your list of functional areas. List below any new functional areas that will need to be developed to support your agency's vision for the future:

1. _____
2. _____
3. _____
4. _____
5. _____
6. _____

Clarify the Purpose of Each Function

Review the two lists of functional areas that you just created, and ask yourself:

1. Are there overlaps in functional services?

2. Could some functional areas be combined to serve a particular need more efficiently?

3. Should some functional areas be divided into new areas?

4. Which functional areas will use the same types of resources (e.g. office equipment, computer hardware and software)?

5. Which functional areas will require identical labor skills?

6. What other similarities or disparities exist in your current and proposed functional areas plan?

FUNCTIONAL AREA PRIMARY PURPOSE DEFINITION

List and identify the primary purpose for each functional area. Make a copy of this page if you need additional space.

Functional Area: _____

       Purpose: _____

                  _____

Functional Area: _____

       Purpose: _____

                  _____

Functional Area: _____

       Purpose: _____

                  _____

Functional Area: _____

       Purpose: _____

                  _____

Functional Area: _____

       Purpose: _____

                  _____

Functional Area: _____

       Purpose: _____

                  _____

DETERMINING THE ROLES FOR EACH FUNCTIONAL AREA

Regardless of how effectively your organization has designed its functional areas plan, there will be overlap between the roles of functional areas. For example:

Functional Area: Human Service Information and Referral

Purpose: Provide information to inquiring callers about appropriate human services

Functional Roles: Educate the community about appropriate human services.

Promote appropriate human services to inquiring callers.

Communicate with the appropriate human services to respond to a specific need.

In this example, the roles of the information and referral functional area overlap with roles of the agency's communications, marketing and public relations departments.

Listing Functional Roles and Areas

Clarify any overlaps by identifying the functional roles of each of your agency's functional areas:

Functional Area and Roles:
Functional Area and Roles:
Functional Area and Roles:
Functional Area and Roles:

SKILL ASSESSMENT FOR EACH ROLE

Now, review the following list of professional skills. Add any other skills that could enhance the effectiveness of your agency's functional roles:

- Agency Knowledge
- Interpersonal Communication Skills
- Administrative and Supervision Skills
- Leadership Skills
- Creativity and Initiative Skills
- Time Management Skills
- Nonprofit Human Resources Knowledge
- Legal Knowledge
- Government Knowledge
- Writing Competencies
- Research, Evaluation and Data Management Skills
- Analytical and Problem-Solving Skills
- Financial and Management Accounting Skills
- Fundraising Knowledge and Skills
- Computer Literacy
- Foreign Language Fluency
- Public Relations Knowledge and Skills
- Marketing Knowledge and Skills
- Construction Skills
- Medical Skills
- Other _____

_____

_____

_____

FUNCTIONAL AREA WORKSHEET

Identify those skills required for each functional area role:

Functional Area Role	Professional Skills Required

VOLUNTEER UTILIZATION THROUGHOUT THE ORGANIZATION

Now you are ready to create a volunteer skills bank. The following questions will help you complete the form on the next page. Make extra copies for additional functional area roles.

1. What functional area roles would benefit from additional volunteer support?

2. What skills are required for prospective volunteers in each functional area?

3. Reference other functional areas within your agency that utilize the same professional skills.

4. Once you have completed forms for all functional roles, job descriptions can be created. These can be used for recruiting prospective volunteers, either within a functional area, or who have a specific skill that would be of benefit to the entire organization. When properly developed and nurtured, volunteer labor can be your agency's most precious resource.

Skills Bank Worksheet

1. Functional Area: _____

2. Skills Required: _____

_____

_____

_____

_____

3. Other Functional Areas That Would Benefit from These Skills:

_____

_____

_____

_____

S E C T I O N

III

Define and Recruit Volunteers

VOLUNTEER JOB DESCRIPTIONS

A comprehensive volunteer recruitment program benefits your organization in many ways:

- Without effective volunteers, you cannot operate a successful agency

- Without volunteers, management of your agency cannot be effective

- Without volunteers to help with clients, your client base will disappear

A well thought out and comprehensive job description will:

- Provide the volunteer with a clear list of responsibilities

- Offer management an evaluation tool for volunteer motivation, direction and discipline

- Communicate to the volunteer that the agency cares

- Provide the volunteer security in knowing what is expected

- Save management time and effort when directing the volunteer's daily activities

SAMPLE JOB DESCRIPTIONS

Sample Job Description For Human Service Information and Referral Volunteer

JOB SUMMARY:

Provide information about appropriate human services to inquiring callers by:

- Gaining more information about the human service needs in the community

- Creating a healthy relationship with clients

- Keeping clients informed about supplementary support services

- Updating the human service database as required

JOB DUTIES:

- Answer the information and referral phone daily

- Actively listen to clients on the phone

- Ask clarifying questions when appropriate

- Provide emotional support during phone calls

- Identify and inform clients about primary services as appropriate to needs

- Identify and inform clients about supplementary support services

- Maintain a telephone log on the number of callers daily and the types of requests

- Update the database and summarize the number and types of requests in a monthly report

- Attend human service planning meetings in the community to learn about new human service programs

- Serve on a community needs assessment committee or human service task force

- Write public relations articles about human service requests and needs

Complete the job description form on the following page for a job in your agency.

Job Description Worksheet

for _____

JOB SUMMARY:

_____

_____

- _____

  _____

- _____

  _____

- _____

  _____

JOB DUTIES:

- _____

  _____

- _____

  _____

- _____

  _____

- _____

  _____

- _____

  _____

- _____

  _____

Sample Preferred Skills and Characteristics for Human Service Information and Referral Volunteer

In addition to the job description, a preferred skills and characteristics profile can:

1. Save interviewing time and insure success in identifying an appropriate volunteer assignment

2. Provide a measurement device for the interview process

3. Identify personality characteristics that are essential for the volunteer's success in a specific role

Consider the following sample of preferred skills and characteristics for the human service information and referral volunteer:

PHYSICAL:

1. Adequate vision and hearing

2. Clear, grammatically pleasant and persuasive speaking voice with an animated tone

3. Maturity and respect for his or her body

EDUCATION:

1. High school graduation, college or business school attendance or graduation

2. Additional courses in interpersonal communications, human services, writing, computers, problem-solving

MENTAL, PERSONAL, AND PSYCHOLOGICAL

1. Inquisitiveness—listens and probes to get critical information

2. Poised—keeps level-head, adapts easily, bounces back after failure

3. Socially adept—easily adjusts to various social situations

4. Intelligent—absorbs and applies new information quickly

5. Self-confident and enthusiastic

6. Positive mental attitude

7. Ability to speak comfortably to a variety of people with various backgrounds

8. High level of personal integrity

Complete the Preferred Skills and Characteristics Form on the following page for the job you described on the Job Description Form.

Preferred Skills and Characteristics Worksheet
for _____

PHYSICAL:

1. _____

2. _____

3. _____

EDUCATION:

1. _____

_____

2. _____

_____

MENTAL, PERSONAL, AND PSYCHOLOGICAL:

1. _____

_____

2. _____

_____

3. _____

_____

4. _____

_____

5. _____

_____

6. _____

_____

7. _____

_____

8. _____

_____

Sample Human Service Information and Referral Volunteer Individual Recruitment Summary Form

VOLUNTEER: _____ **DATE:** _____

Suggested Characteristics and Skills

Physical   **Has**   **Not**

1. Adequate Vision   _____   _____
2. Adequate Hearing   _____   _____
3. Speaking Voice   _____   _____
4. Maturity   _____   _____
5. High School Graduate   _____   _____
6. Intelligent (Perceptive)   _____   _____
7. Self-Confident and Enthusiastic   _____   _____
8. High Level of Personal Integrity   _____   _____

Mental, Personal and Psychological	**Low**									**High**
1. Inquisitiveness	1	2	3	4	5	6	7	8	9	10
2. Poised	1	2	3	4	5	6	7	8	9	10
3. Socially Adept	1	2	3	4	5	6	7	8	9	10
4. Positive Mental Attitude	1	2	3	4	5	6	7	8	9	10
5. Ability to Speak Comfortably With a Variety of People	1	2	3	4	5	6	7	8	9	10
6. Human Service Knowledge	1	2	3	4	5	6	7	8	9	10
7. Writing Competencies	1	2	3	4	5	6	7	8	9	10
8. Analytical	1	2	3	4	5	6	7	8	9	10
9. Computer Literacy	1	2	3	4	5	6	7	8	9	10
10. Public Relations Knowledge	1	2	3	4	5	6	7	8	9	10

Does the volunteer possess 75% of the attributes listed?

YES _____   NO _____

Individual Recruitment Summary Worksheet
for _____

VOLUNTEER: _____   DATE: _____

Suggested Characteristics and Skills

Physical   **Has**   **Not**

1. _____   _____
2. _____   _____
3. _____   _____
4. _____   _____
5. _____   _____
6. _____   _____
7. _____   _____
8. _____   _____

Mental, Personal and Psychological   **Low**   **High**

1. 1 2 3 4 5 6 7 8 9 10
2. 1 2 3 4 5 6 7 8 9 10
3. 1 2 3 4 5 6 7 8 9 10
4. 1 2 3 4 5 6 7 8 9 10
5. 1 2 3 4 5 6 7 8 9 10
6. 1 2 3 4 5 6 7 8 9 10
7. 1 2 3 4 5 6 7 8 9 10
8. 1 2 3 4 5 6 7 8 9 10
9. 1 2 3 4 5 6 7 8 9 10
10. 1 2 3 4 5 6 7 8 9 10

Does the volunteer possess 75% of the attributes listed?

YES _____   NO _____

37

Recruiting Volunteers

MULTICULTURAL RECRUITMENT SENSITIVITY

Consider the multicultural needs of your community when assigning a volunteer to a specific job.

Once you determine the cultural demographics of your community, aggressively recruit appropriate minority volunteers. Always maintain demographic balance when hiring agency staff and recruiting agency volunteers.

Consider the following when recruiting minority populations:

- Cultural values and perceptions vary.

- Various cultures view human support services differently. Some cultures are uncomfortable with counseling support services. Other cultures view death as a time to celebrate rather than grieve.

- Certain communication styles within the American culture are offensive to other cultures. For example, maintaining eye contact for extended periods is considered impolite by a number of other cultures.

- Certain personality traits (e.g. inquisitiveness, enthusiasm) are perceived as rude and disrespectful in some other cultures.

Review the following benefits of multicultural recruitment:

- An agency's programs can most easily be adapted to the individual needs of clients when a diverse set of volunteers is available.

- Minority volunteers bridge the cultural gaps among paid staff.

- Cultural understanding within an organization improves when the support team is culturally diverse.

- Cultural diversity empowers people to explore human services and community issues in new ways.

- Diversity breeds innovation and a realistic, appropriate vision for the future.

VOLUNTEER RECRUITMENT SOURCES

Once you have defined job responsibilities and qualifications for a specific volunteer function, you can recruit volunteers through:

Internal Organizational Networking
Community Networking
Company Community Service Projects
Volunteer Information and Referral Services
Rehabilitation Training Programs
Trade or Job Retraining Programs
Work Experience Candidates
School Project Contracts
Educational Internships
Collaborative Partnerships

Internal Organizational Networking

Internal organizational networking empowers current volunteers to recruit specific community members with specialized skills. To identify an individual for a specific function, ask all volunteers, staff and agency associates if they know anyone who can perform a particular function. Consider the following:

- An agency volunteer who asks his neighbor, a contractor, to help remodel the agency's bathroom

- A staff member who asks a marketing consultant to help write a volunteer recruitment manual

- An agency auditor who asks his associates to provide volunteer bookkeeping services to the agency

- An agency volunteer who asks her friend, a graphic artist, to help design the agency service brochure

Identify three personal contacts you know who can provide specific and unique voluntary services to your agency:

Contact Name	Specific and Unique Service
1. _____	_____
2. _____	_____
3. _____	_____

COMMUNITY NETWORKING

Ongoing community networking is a powerful volunteer recruitment strategy. Volunteer networking opportunities are incorporated easily into an agency's daily operations. Consider the following:

- At a community presentation, an agency representative meets members of the audience and shares volunteer opportunity information with those who express interest.

- At a social gathering, an agency employee discusses his or her job with a couple of people, who then express interest in participating in the agency's programs. The employee later contacts these people to discuss volunteer opportunities.

- You know that local merchants are interested in promoting youth development activities. You approach the merchants for fund-raising donations and support for your agency's youth development programs.

- You approach acquaintances who take care of senior parents, for volunteer assistance with your agency's health services for seniors.

- Your friend who works at a computer software company, expresses interest in your agency's use of computers. You approach him for technical computer assistance.

As these examples illustrate, networking relationships are created through formal and informal opportunities. The critical elements present in any healthy networking relationship include:

- Mutual respect

- Honesty

- Clear communication

- Risk taking and assertiveness

- Willingness to share information and resources

COMMUNITY NETWORKING EXERCISE

As you answer the following questions, think about the last social event you attended. It might have been an informal social gathering, a sporting activity, a neighborhood or school event.

1. Who did you talk with?

_____

_____

_____

_____

2. Did you talk with anyone about human services or your agency's programs? Who were those people?

_____

_____

_____

3. Did anyone talk to you about their job or interests? Who were those people? Would your agency benefit from any of their interests or expertise?

_____

_____

_____

4. Recalling the event, is there anyone who you might approach now about a volunteer opportunity?

_____

_____

_____

5. How and when will you approach each of these individuals?

_____

_____

_____

COMPANY COMMUNITY SERVICE PROJECTS

In addition to participating in human service collaborative projects, some larger companies have community service departments or participate in specific community service projects. When recruiting a company's volunteers, the company may also donate other resources for a community service project. Examples of company community services include:

- A company fund or foundation that provides specific human service financial support

- A product donation program for nonprofit organizations

- Initial or ongoing financial support for a nonprofit community service (e.g. a children's discovery museum, a historical museum)

- Initial or ongoing financial support for a specific community event

- Participation in community planning and problem-solving task force committees

- Free facility usage for nonprofit groups

- Loaned labor and donated materials for specific community projects

Company Community Service Project Worksheet

In the space provided, design a company community service project that you might propose for your agency. Identify volunteer services that would be required, and any other resources a company might donate for the project.

Project Title: _____

Required Volunteer Services:

_____

_____

_____

_____

Other Company Resources That Might Be Donated:

_____

_____

VOLUNTEER INFORMATION AND REFERRAL SERVICES

Volunteer commitment is flourishing as a result of depleting public funding and the resurgence of community altruism. Progressive companies provide flexible work schedules for employees who want to participate in volunteer activities. One employee may work one morning a week in his child's school. Another may teach vocational computer skills to economically disadvantaged adults.

Volunteer information and referral services provide prospective volunteers with information about volunteer opportunities in the community. The greatest challenge for these organizations is to help nonprofit organizations create stimulating volunteer opportunities for committed community members.

Volunteer information and referral services are available through:

- Non Profit Agencies

- College Placement Offices

- Employment Development Offices

- Community Recreation Centers

- Libraries

- Schools

Once you identify your community's volunteer information and referral services, you can submit completed job descriptions with preferred skills and characteristics to the volunteer service. The service will post the volunteer opportunities on their volunteer board.

Initially, it is best to simplify a job description. More volunteers will be qualified to apply for the volunteer opportunity when the job is simply defined. For example, a simplified job description for a human service information and referral volunteer might include one of the following:

- Telephone Contact Work

- Support Counseling

- Data Entry

- Data Reporting

JOB TITLE OPPORTUNITIES AND RESPONSIBILITIES

Refer back to one of the volunteer job description forms you created earlier. In the space provided below, simplify the job into four distinct opportunities. List each distinct opportunity with its specific responsibilities.

Job Description Title: _____

1. Distinct Opportunity: _____

   Responsibilities: _____

   _____

   _____

   _____

   _____

2. Distinct Opportunity: _____

   Responsibilities: _____

   _____

   _____

   _____

   _____

3. Distinct Opportunity: _____

   Responsibilities: _____

   _____

   _____

   _____

   _____

4. Distinct Opportunity: _____

   Responsibilities: _____

   _____

   _____

   _____

   _____

REHABILITATION TRAINING

Rehabilitative vocational training has expanded in recent years as more people survive serious injuries. In addition, personal computers have provided new occupational opportunities for the orthopedically handicapped.

Public schools and private nonprofit agencies currently provide rehabilitative vocational training. These programs assess the client's limitations and abilities, and design an individual learning plan for the client. As appropriate, each plan includes learning basic living skills, learning adaptive behaviors to overcome physical and mental limitations, career counseling and training.

Most career training programs include skill acquisition, social development, effective job hunting skills and practical work experiences. Practical work experiences are provided in sheltered workshops and through community placements.

Rehabilitative vocational training programs include:

- Computer Programming and Data Entry

- Clerical Services

- Production Assembly

- Food Services

- Custodial

- Retail

Anyone interested in providing rehabilitation training or work experiences should contact local and state rehabilitation programs and nonprofit programs.

Identify three rehabilitative training or volunteer work experiences you can provide in your agency:

_____

_____

_____

_____

_____

TRADE OR JOB RETRAINING

As the specialized demands for labor increase, vocational training programs, adult education centers and colleges are creatively adjusting their curriculum and programs to meet the needs. A major element in each program addresses how to apply newly acquired skills to actual work experience.

Nonprofit organizations can design appropriate work experiences for this special population. Trade or job retraining work experiences can include:

- Facility repair, remodeling and construction projects

- Computer programming and data entry

- Bookkeeping and accounting support services

- Program support services (e.g. food services, elder care, child care, health services)

- Legal support services

- Graphic arts support

- Public relations and marketing support

- Fund raising support and strategic planning

- Clerical services

- Custodial services

Circle three services on this list that your agency could benefit from. In the spaces below, list three more services that could be provided to your agency:

1. _____

_____

2. _____

_____

3. _____

_____

WORK EXPERIENCE DOCUMENTATION

Work experience documentation is required of anyone who applies for a job. Volunteer work experience can provide the required documentation. The following biographies illustrate how volunteer work experiences can significantly change people's careers.

BIOGRAPHY 1: Janell, The Teacher

From the time she was in high school, Janell dreamed of becoming a teacher. She entered college as a teaching major, but became discouraged when she learned that teaching jobs were limited. After much deliberation, Janell dropped out of college, worked in industry and gave birth to two children.

After years of volunteering in parent participation nursery schools, Janell was offered a part-time teaching position at the local adult education center. Later, she returned to college and completed her undergraduate and graduate education.

BIOGRAPHY 2: Faye, The Counselor

While at home full-time, raising her four children, Faye was the neighborhood "mom" who friends turned to for advice. In addition, she volunteered at a women's shelter. After becoming a single parent, she explored various career options. By receiving student financial aid, Faye was able to enter college and complete her graduate degree in family counseling.

BIOGRAPHY 3: Fred, The Accountant

Fred always enjoyed numbers. After high school, he worked as a production control planner. He also served as treasurer for a local service group. Inspired by his volunteer experience, he returned to college and became an accountant.

BIOGRAPHY 4: Roger, The Electrician

Roger liked to work on home projects. In addition, when he had the opportunity to help with stage construction for local school plays, he installed the stage lights. Based upon his volunteer experiences, he enrolled in a trade school and became an electrician.

IN-HOUSE VOLUNTEER BIOGRAPHIES

Consider how volunteers in your agency have been affected by their volunteer experiences. Write four biographies about changes volunteers have made in their careers or their lives after working at your agency.

If you do not have volunteer examples within your agency, consider how you and your friends have been affected by various volunteer experiences.

BIOGRAPHY 1:

BIOGRAPHY 2:

BIOGRAPHY 3:

BIOGRAPHY 4:

SCHOOL PROJECT CONTRACTS

School project contracts with nonprofit organizations are uniquely designed to meet the needs of the organizations involved. The following are examples of school project contracts:

1. An agency sponsors a contest with a local high school art department to design an agency logo, to make posters for a fund-raising event, or to design the agency's public relations art work. Winning entries receive donated prizes and newspaper recognition.

2. Elementary school students stuff envelopes for the agency's major fund-raising event. The school is recognized for its unique contribution to the community.

3. Elementary and high school students help a local service group clean local parks for a day.

4. School groups provide friendly visits and entertainment to local nursing homes and hospitals.

5. School groups serve meals at a local homeless shelter.

6. A school class adopts a disadvantaged family for the year, and provides the family with special treats on holidays.

7. Schools provide ongoing clerical support to local nonprofit organizations.

8. Schools provide labor support at fund-raising events.

9. Schools assist nonprofit organizations in human service research.

10. Students provide labor support at child care centers.

11. Students assist the disabled with daily housekeeping chores.

12. Students serve on community commissions and task force committees.

13. A company pays a vocational class to provide a service.

14. Students write newspaper articles for an agency.

SCHOOL PROJECT CONTRACTS (continued)

Consider the unique service needs of your nonprofit organization, and review the volunteer skills bank you created earlier. In the space below, identify ten project contracts that you can create with local schools.

Do not feel inhibited when designing your options. As nonprofit budgets shrink, local schools are becoming more committed to having students support the human service needs of their community.

School Project Contracts for My Nonprofit Organization

1. _____

2. _____

3. _____

4. _____

5. _____

6. _____

7. _____

8. _____

9. _____

10. _____

EDUCATIONAL INTERNSHIPS

In recent years, many human service volunteers have been recruited through educational internships. Educational internships provide academic credits to students completing specific work experiences. Educational internships can be developed in the following ways:

University Graduate Educational Internships

1. A nonprofit agency contacts a local university about a prospective volunteer opportunity.

2. After gathering preliminary information about the internship, the university refers the agency to the appropriate graduate department.

3. Most requests for counseling services are referred to the graduate school of psychology. Other referrals are made to the graduate schools of education, business, law, and public administration.

4. Once an agency identifies the appropriate department, the agency is asked to complete university internship request forms.

5. A stipend may be requested to cover transportation and other basic expenses.

6. Once the completed forms are submitted to the university, the university determines if the request will fulfill the department's program requirements.

7. If the request meets the university's requirements, an internship announcement about the volunteer opportunity is posted on the internship bulletin board.

8. Once the internship assignment has been finalized, the nonprofit organization signs an agreement with the school. The agency agrees to provide the student with an appropriate academic experience and to provide performance feedback to the academic advisor.

EDUCATIONAL INTERNSHIPS (continued)

Benefits: Most graduate interns tend to be highly motivated and capable. University graduate internships range from one academic quarter through an entire academic year.

Limits: The nonprofit organization must fulfill its educational commitment to the university and provide appropriate support and resources.

Undergraduate Educational Internships

1. The undergraduate internship's application process is similar to the graduate internship.

2. Fewer academic commitments are required for the nonprofit agency when compared to the graduate internship.

Benefits: The duration of an undergraduate internship ranges from one academic quarter to an entire academic year, depending on the academic major and the college. Nonprofit commitments to the college are less demanding than for graduate internships.

Limits: Undergraduate students need more supervision and development than graduate students.

High School Educational Internships

1. High school internships are documented work experiences within the community to fulfill specific academic requirements.

2. High school internships include community service work experiences for a guidance, psychology or social studies class, and child development experiences for a child development class.

3. Local companies offer high school internships to students to develop specialized skills or explore a particular career. Computer companies offer summer jobs to prospective engineers. Work study opportunities can be created to meet individual student's needs.

COLLABORATIVE PARTNERSHIPS

As nonprofit funding and community resources become strained, community collaborative partnerships are being designed creatively to:

- Utilize community funding and resources effectively

- Promote cooperative community problem-solving between government agencies, nonprofit agencies and businesses

- Exchange ideas and resources between nonprofit entities and local businesses

- Encourage commitment and support in meeting a community's human service needs

- Nurture altruism within the community

Collaboration and partnership are essential when designing objectives to meet community needs.

For each of the following three collaborative partnership examples, identify the participating groups and the function of each group. Then, create a collaborative partnership that would benefit your agency.

1. A company sponsors an ongoing mentorship program for disadvantaged youth from a local school. The students meet their mentors weekly at the workplace. A local fast food restaurant provides catered snacks at these meetings.

   Partner #1: _____

   Function: _____

   Partner #2: _____

   Function: _____

   Partner #3: _____

   Function: _____

COLLABORATIVE PARTNERSHIPS (continued)

2. A local school and senior center provide child care labor and recreational activities for a child development center at a local work site.

Partner #1: _____

Function: _____

Partner #2: _____

Function: _____

Partner #3: _____

Function: _____

Partner #4: _____

Function: _____

3. A nonprofit agency receives computer hardware for ABC Computer Company. TVE Software Company donates software and GBA Associates provides technical assistance to set up the system. MPM Accounting and Bookkeeping Services creates computer accounting procedures.

Partner #1: _____

Function: _____

Partner #2: _____

Function: _____

Partner #3: _____

Function: _____

Partner #4: _____

Function: _____

Partner #5: _____

Function: _____

COLLABORATIVE PARTNERSHIP FUNCTIONS

Your agency's proposed collaborative partnership:

_____

_____

_____

_____

_____

_____

_____

_____

_____

_____

Partner #1: _____

Function: _____

Partner #2: _____

Function: _____

Partner #3: _____

Function: _____

Partner #4: _____

Function: _____

EFFECTIVE STRATEGIES FOR INTERVIEWING VOLUNTEERS

Most prospective volunteers are interviewed initially on the phone. A telephone interview can measure how a volunteer presents him or herself on the phone, and the prospective volunteer can determine whether he or she is interested in volunteering for the organization.

Basic characteristics to listen for during the initial telephone discussion include:

► A pleasant voice and manner—clients cannot see the volunteer during a phone conversation. Listen for the prospective volunteer's pitch, tone, inflection, volume and clarity.

► Language skills—determine if the prospective volunteer uses proper English and how well he or she communicates.

► Decide if the prospective volunteer has a real desire to work in your agency.

► Enthusiasm—a positive attitude is contagious.

► Listening ability—studies show that 40 to 60 percent of a person's day should be spent listening.

The telephone interview is intended to keep the prospective volunteer relaxed and talking long enough for you to examine his or her voice for:

- Excitement
- Control
- Inflection
- Sincerity
- Empathy
- Professionalism
- Listening ability
- Commitment
- Command of language
- Clarity

THE VOLUNTEER TELEPHONE INTERVIEW

These questions are usually appropriate during the telephone interview:

1. What do you like best about your job?

2. What are your previous volunteer experiences?

3. What do you do in your spare time?

4. What interests you most about this human service agency?

5. What did you like best about school?

6. If you could do anything for employment, what would you do and why?

7. Tell me about growing up—what significant events do you remember? What specific incidents occurred that made an impression?

8. If you had one wish for human services, what would it be?

9. If you could do anything, what would you do for your community?

10. When considering human service needs, what is your vision for the future?

SAMPLE QUESTIONNAIRE

Telephone Interview Questionnaire for Volunteers

Volunteer's Name: _____   **Phone:** _____

Address: _____   **City:** _____

1. What jobs or volunteer experiences have you enjoyed?

   _____   _____

   _____   _____

2. What was your first position in a job or volunteer experience?

   _____

3. What did you want to accomplish in your first job or volunteer experience?

   _____

4. What do you or would you like most out of a volunteer opportunity?

   _____

5. What kind of personal satisfaction do you want to accomplish in any job or volunteer experience?

   _____

6. What would you be willing to do in this volunteer experience that you have never done before?

   _____

7. What would you need to overcome to make this happen?

   _____

8. What do you like best about our agency?

   _____

9. What questions or comments do you have?

   _____

Sample Telephone Interview Checklist
for Volunteers

Volunteer's Name: _____ Interviewer: _____

Circle the appropriate numerical value for each item.

		Low									High
1.	Excitement	1	2	3	4	5	6	7	8	9	10
2.	Control	1	2	3	4	5	6	7	8	9	10
3.	Inflection	1	2	3	4	5	6	7	8	9	10
4.	Sincerity	1	2	3	4	5	6	7	8	9	10
5.	Empathy	1	2	3	4	5	6	7	8	9	10
6.	Professionalism	1	2	3	4	5	6	7	8	9	10
7.	Listening ability	1	2	3	4	5	6	7	8	9	10
8.	Commitment	1	2	3	4	5	6	7	8	9	10
9.	Command of language	1	2	3	4	5	6	7	8	9	10
10.	Clarity	1	2	3	4	5	6	7	8	9	10

Comments: _____

_____

_____

_____

_____

_____

Considering the telephone interview, the prospective volunteer is (circle only one):

Unsatisfactory   Satisfactory   Above Average   Excellent

Worksheet for Volunteer Telephone Interview Checklist

Volunteer's Name: _____ **Interviewer:** _____

Please list basic characteristics that you intend to listen for during your initial telephone interview. Circle the appropriate numerical value for each item.

	Low									**High**
1. _____	1	2	3	4	5	6	7	8	9	10
2. _____	1	2	3	4	5	6	7	8	9	10
3. _____	1	2	3	4	5	6	7	8	9	10
4. _____	1	2	3	4	5	6	7	8	9	10
5. _____	1	2	3	4	5	6	7	8	9	10
6. _____	1	2	3	4	5	6	7	8	9	10
7. _____	1	2	3	4	5	6	7	8	9	10
8. _____	1	2	3	4	5	6	7	8	9	10
9. _____	1	2	3	4	5	6	7	8	9	10
10. _____	1	2	3	4	5	6	7	8	9	10

Comments: _____

_____

_____

_____

_____

_____

Considering the telephone interview, the prospective volunteer is (circle only one):

    Unsatisfactory   Satisfactory   Above Average   Excellent

THE VOLUNTEER PERSONAL INTERVIEW

Once you have completed the preliminary telephone interview, invite the prospective volunteer to an interview in person with you and your agency's staff. The in-person interview will give you a chance to examine a volunteer's appearance and how he or she presents him or herself. It can also help you identify factors about the volunteer that can be significant in his or her agency role. Examples include:

- The prospective volunteer's motivation

- How the volunteer deals with rejection

- His or her attitude about the proposed volunteer opportunity

- His or her career expectations

- The prospective volunteer's compassion

When interviewing, ask questions that require more than a ''yes'' or a ''no'' answer. Measure how the prospective volunteer will perform his or her job by asking situational, task-related questions. Examples for a human service information and referral volunteer include:

- When responding to a telephone request for temporary shelter, the volunteer is told by the wife that the husband physically abuses their children. How would the volunteer handle the situation?

- A phone caller is incoherent and sounds like she is severely emotionally disturbed. How would the volunteer handle the situation?

- A phone caller is irate because no more rental assistance emergency funds are available. How would the volunteer handle the situation?

- Why should the volunteer be assigned to this opportunity?

- What additional skills would the volunteer like to develop for this opportunity?

THE VOLUNTEER PERSONAL INTERVIEW (continued)

Structured interviews help identify prospective volunteers who have skills required for success. Ask each prospective volunteer the same interview questions. You can then compare prospective volunteers' responses and determine the most appropriate candidate for a specific assignment.

File back-up notes in your files, in the event a prospective volunteer expresses concerns about the way that he or she was treated during the interview process. The structured interview provides additional tools to make the interview productive and less time consuming.

Following are sample structured interview questions:

Work Experiences:

1. How did you find your current job or your most recent volunteer opportunity?

2. What do you like most about your job or volunteer opportunity?

3. What do you do on an average work day?

4. How often do you work with others?

5. Do you prefer working alone or in small groups?

6. How do you get along with your supervisor?

7. What does your supervisor appreciate most about you?

8. When have you received criticism?

9. What are five adjectives that describe your company or agency?

10. What is your greatest professional accomplishment?

11. What do you not like about your current job or most recent volunteer experience?

12. What major obstacle have you overcome in your present company or volunteer opportunity?

13. How does a volunteer opportunity with our agency fit with your career goals?

14. What type of volunteer training do you expect from us?

15. What else can we offer you to enhance your experience with us?

16. How long do you plan to work at our agency?

17. Describe the perfect supervisor.

Education:

1. How many units have you completed in college?

2. What were your major and minor in college?

3. How did you select the college you attended?

4. What college/high school class did you enjoy the most? Why?

5. Describe your favorite teacher.

6. What college/high school class did you hate? Why?

7. What was the most valuable lesson you learned in school?

8. What did you do during your summer vacations?

9. What do you miss most about school?

10. If you could live your life over, how would you change your educational experiences?

Personal Factors:

1. How would you best describe yourself?

2. What are your hobbies?

3. What do you enjoy most about life?

4. What are your strengths?

5. If you could live your life over, what would you change?

6. What did you like best about being a child?

7. What frustrates you the most?

8. What do you think is your greatest weakness?

9. If you could do anything in the world, what would you do?

10. When considering your career, where do you see yourself five and ten years from now?

Summary Question:

1. Do you have any questions about this volunteer opportunity at our agency?

2. What else would you like to tell me about yourself?

Sample Personal Interview Checklist

Volunteer's Name: _____ **Interviewer:** _____

Circle the appropriate numerical value for each item.

		Low									**High**
1.	Motivation	1	2	3	4	5	6	7	8	9	10
2.	Ability to deal with rejection	1	2	3	4	5	6	7	8	9	10
3.	Positive attitude about human services	1	2	3	4	5	6	7	8	9	10
4.	Solid volunteer expectations	1	2	3	4	5	6	7	8	9	10
5.	Compassion	1	2	3	4	5	6	7	8	9	10
6.	Ability to handle job situations	1	2	3	4	5	6	7	8	9	10
7.	Composure under pressure	1	2	3	4	5	6	7	8	9	10
8.	Quick thinker	1	2	3	4	5	6	7	8	9	10
9.	Enjoys people	1	2	3	4	5	6	7	8	9	10
10.	Listening skills	1	2	3	4	5	6	7	8	9	10

Comments: _____

_____

_____

_____

_____

_____

When considering the personal interview, the prospective volunteer is (circle one):

Unsatisfactory   Satisfactory   Above Average   Excellent

Worksheet for Personal Interview Checklist

Volunteer's Name: _____ Interviewer: _____

List required or preferred volunteer characteristics you observe during the personal interview. Circle the appropriate numerical value for each item.

	Low									High
1. _____	1	2	3	4	5	6	7	8	9	10
2. _____	1	2	3	4	5	6	7	8	9	10
3. _____	1	2	3	4	5	6	7	8	9	10
4. _____	1	2	3	4	5	6	7	8	9	10
5. _____	1	2	3	4	5	6	7	8	9	10
6. _____	1	2	3	4	5	6	7	8	9	10
7. _____	1	2	3	4	5	6	7	8	9	10
8. _____	1	2	3	4	5	6	7	8	9	10
9. _____	1	2	3	4	5	6	7	8	9	10
10. _____	1	2	3	4	5	6	7	8	9	10

Comments: _____

_____

_____

_____

_____

_____

When considering the personal interview, the prospective volunteer is (circle one):

    Unsatisfactory   Satisfactory   Above Average   Excellent

VOLUNTEER AGREEMENTS AND CONTRACTS

After completing the personal interview, discuss the following information before finalizing the volunteer agreement or contract:

- The agency's policy on business expense reimbursement

- Volunteer benefits (e.g. free meals, free computer usage, agency program discounts)

- Stipends

- Training programs

- Growth opportunities

- Educational opportunities

- Volunteer recognition program

- Agency contests

- Agency cultural and social activities

- Agency's work hours, holiday schedule, security policy, parking permits, etc.

Sell the benefits of working at your agency. Assure the volunteer his or her experience at your agency will be stimulating, rewarding and challenging. Give the volunteer a tour of the agency and introduce him or her to the staff: make the volunteer feel like one of the family.

After answering any questions the volunteer may have about your agency, clarify all agreements about job responsibilities, work hours and supervisor assignment; sign documentation or contracts required for educational internships or work experience.

S E C T I O N

IV

Volunteer Assignment and Development

Match the Assignment with the Volunteer's Skills

Once the volunteer is assigned to a specific job, adjust the job to the volunteer's current skill level. As the volunteer becomes more competent in the job, his or her volunteer assignment can be modified. If you acquire a volunteer who is highly qualified for the current position, as time permits, allow the volunteer to creatively expand the job responsibilities.

STRUCTURING AND RESTRUCTURING AVAILABLE VOLUNTEER OPPORTUNITIES

In the space below, outline how you would adjust a current volunteer opportunity at your agency for a volunteer with minimal skill competencies, and how you would expand the same opportunity for a graduate student or a highly qualified volunteer.

Job Title: _____

Current Job Responsibilities:

_____

_____

_____

_____

_____

Minimal Job Responsibilities:

_____

_____

_____

_____

Expanded Job Responsibilities:

_____

_____

_____

_____

DEVELOP THE VOLUNTEER'S WORKPLAN

After assessing a volunteer's specific skills, ask the volunteer to develop a workplan on how he or she plans to meet the primary and supplementary job duties. They should include specific time periods and methods of evaluation for completing individual work activities.

Discuss the plan with the volunteer after the volunteer completes the workplan. Explore other options to enhance the volunteer's work experiences while with your agency. At regularly scheduled meetings, modify the workplan as appropriate.

Sample Workplan

Review and complete the following sample workplan for a specific volunteer's job within your agency. List and define each job duty separately. If the job includes more than two job duties, make additional copies of this form.

WORKPLAN FOR 1992–93

Job Summary: _____

_____

_____

Job Duty: _____

Supporting Activities	Time	Evaluation
_____	_____	_____
_____	_____	_____
_____	_____	_____

Job Duty: _____

Supporting Activities	Time	Evaluation
_____	_____	_____
_____	_____	_____
_____	_____	_____

WORK CARDS AND TRAINING MATERIALS

Job work cards and agency training materials simplify the new volunteer orientation process. Post a job work card, including the following information, in the volunteer's work area:

- Brief job description
- Summary of job duties
- Actual times that certain activities occur
- Names and phone numbers of emergency contacts
- General safety rules
- Agency's disaster evacuation plan

Agency training materials can assist staff in training new volunteers. Training materials can include:

- Outline of the agency's mission, history and long-range plan
- Organizational chart of staff and volunteer support positions
- General description of each agency program
- Overview of the clients' needs and characteristics
- Review of agency procedures
- Guidelines on how to effectively serve clients
- Skill training modules for specific jobs
- Overview on how to be an effective agency volunteer

Training materials can be presented to volunteers in many ways, including:

- Volunteer training books for specific volunteer jobs
- Job skill workbooks
- Flip charts
- Overheads
- Icebreakers
- Work-team skill development activities
- Role-plays
- Performing arts activities
- Games
- Brainstorming activities

AGENCY VOLUNTEER TRAINING MATERIALS EVALUATION

1. Have you developed work cards for volunteer jobs?

2. If you have work cards, what information is currently listed? If you do not have work cards, what information would you list on the cards if you had them?

3. What volunteer or staff training materials does your agency currently use for orientations?

4. What volunteer training materials do you need to develop?

5. In what other creative ways can you communicate training information to volunteers?

6. What books does your agency have to help create innovative training materials?

7. What community resources can help to develop creative training materials?

8. Who is creative on your staff, including volunteers?

9. What agencies can share training resources?

10. What have you learned about your agency from this evaluation?

COMMUNICATION AND LISTENING SKILLS TRAINING

An agency prospers when staff members, volunteers and clients communicate effectively. Effective communication occurs when a mutual understanding of information is shared between two or more people. To enhance effective communications, an agency should provide ongoing communication and listening skills training for staff and volunteers.

When developing auditory training presentations, consider the three basic levels of listening:

MARGINAL LISTENING occurs when communicating with new people or when the communicator concentrates on what he or she is going to say next.

EVALUATIVE LISTENING takes place when a person is not concentrating on the meaning of what is being said or is influenced by past history. It is also a problem when the speaker is interrupted.

ACTIVE LISTENING occurs when the speaker's viewpoint is understood and when the listener focuses complete attention on the speaker's feelings and thoughts.

The following guidelines increase effective auditory presentations:

- The speaker should discourage side conversations.

- The speaker should consider the audience, and attempt to understand their points of view.

- The speaker should include specific time(s) for questions during the presentation.

- The speaker should discourage interruptions during the presentation.

- Audience members should concentrate on what the speaker is saying.

- Audience members should confirm what they hear.

- Audience members should not assume they know what the speaker is going to say.

- Audience members should listen for overtones in what is being said.

COMMUNICATION AND LISTENING SKILLS TRAINING (continued)

Clarifying questions focus on what the speaker is thinking, can influence the speaker and accomplish the following:

- Uncover the audience's needs

- Create mutual understanding

- Clarify the speaker's viewpoint

- Identify the speaker's values

Consider the four basic types of questions:

1. **CLOSED QUESTIONS** are used to gain agreement and can be answered with a simple yes or no and begin with do, is, are, can, will and could.

2. **OPEN-ENDED QUESTIONS** are used to gain information and begin with who, what, where, when, why or how.

3. **REFLECTIVE QUESTIONS** acknowledge what the speaker has said and provide a method for correctly interpreting the speaker's statement.

4. **DIRECTIVE QUESTIONS** are used to influence a person toward your viewpoint and suggest dissatisfaction or an alternative solution.

Effective communication processes build and enhance healthy relationships.

LEADERSHIP AND TEAM BUILDING

Effective leadership builds an organization's team to cooperatively achieve its mission. A successful leader gains support through interactions with others, by offering the means to satisfy perceived needs. Review the following leadership characteristics:

- **Knowledge** = componential intelligence required to gain power

- **Experience** = creative insight required to employ the appropriate tactic

- **Vision** = inspirational transfer of knowledge and experience to gain the content

- **Charisma** = presentation of power, tactic and content

Effective leadership is, then, the impact of acceptance gained by employing power, tactic, and content.

What Makes a Good Leader?

Answer the following questions about a leader that you respect:

1. How experienced and knowledgeable is this leader in his or her job?

2. How does this leader communicate with and respond to others?

3. How do others relate to this leader's example?

4. Does this leader have vision? If so, how far into the future is this leader's vision?

5. What do you admire most about this leader?

6. What frustrates you about this leader?

7. How does this leader compare to other historical leaders in our country?

8. What can you learn from this leader?

LEADERSHIP AND TEAM BUILDING (continued)

Teambuilding occurs when members of a group strive to work together respectfully to achieve a goal. Consider facilitating the following activities intended to foster trust, respect, cooperation and teambuilding:

1. Give a group a puzzle to solve. The group must solve the puzzle through physical manipulation—talking is not allowed.

2. Organize a scavenger hunt in which the group must collect a list of articles within a limited time.

3. Instruct the group to divide up into pairs. Blindfold one partner. The other partner is instructed to lead the blindfolded partner on a hike.

4. Break the group into small groups of three to five people. Give each small group one pair of scissors, a set of marking pens, and one large sheet of paper. Each group completes a functional agency goal using only these limited resources.

5. Each agency member must contribute a unique talent at the annual picnic.

6. Describe an event to the group. Assign roles to various group members who must act out the end of the story.

7. Give a group one sack of groceries. Tell them this is the only food they will have for a week. Have the group decide how they will use their limited resources.

8. Within a limited time, have small groups design logos for your agency. When the logos are completed, have each group describe their logo to the larger group. Vote on the winning entry.

9. Lay a large sheet of butcher paper on a table. Divide the group into two. Have one group design a pictorial representation of your agency. Then ask the other group to describe the pictures.

10. Write a story with blank spaces to be filled in. Describe the missing words and have group members decide on appropriate words. Weave these words into the story while reading the story to the group.

ONGOING TRAINING OPPORTUNITIES

Effective agencies provide ongoing training opportunities for all agency staff and volunteers, sometimes on a weekly or monthly basis, while other times far more sporadically. The following is considered to be the best collection of practices for developing staff and volunteers:

1. The trainer is competent and has expertise in adult learning theories.

2. Effective training strategies are modelled, which focus on learning methodology.

3. Training is systemized, standardized and adaptive. It utilizes technological aids.

4. Participants collaborate in planning goals and activities that respond to assessed needs.

5. Training integrates holistically all elements and functions within the agency.

6. Training is a complex and ambitious long-term process.

7. Training is an integral part of the agency.

8. Training is offered at convenient times and locations.

9. Training encourages voluntary participation.

10. Training is relevant and includes individualized programs.

11. Training includes demonstrations, practice and feedback.

12. Theory, modeling, practice, feedback and activity coaching are part of the training.

13. Training provides small group learning and allows participant feedback.

14. Training emphasizes motivation and enculturation.

15. Training emphasizes career-long growth and sufficient allocation of resources.

16. The training includes peer coaching.

17. The evaluation is collaborative.

YOUR TRAINING DEVELOPMENT PROGRAM

Answer the following questions about your current training development program:

1. How does your agency currently provide training?

2. When you reviewed the list of best training development practices, what did you identify as your agency's strengths?

3. What training practices does your agency need to develop further?

4. List twelve training modules for your agency.

5. What overlaps exist in your agency's training?

6. When considering development training, what community resources can your agency benefit from?

7. Who do you most admire when considering nonprofit employees?

8. List characteristics you most admire in this nonprofit employee.

9. How can you further develop these characteristics in yourself?

10. How can you help others develop these characteristics?

WEEKLY VOLUNTEER SUPPORT MEETINGS

Weekly volunteer support meetings offer many opportunities for volunteers. During the meetings, volunteers can:

▶ Share common volunteer experiences

▶ Brainstorm and problem-solve volunteer concerns

▶ Receive ongoing volunteer training

▶ Learn more about the agency and its programs

▶ Receive skill development training

▶ Participate in social events with agency staff

▶ Participate in guest speaker presentations

▶ Share career goals and inspire each other

▶ Receive recognition for their outstanding work

Scheduling meetings can present a real challenge. Some agencies have found that weekly night meetings are best for volunteers. Their meetings are scheduled from 5:00 p.m. until 6:00 p.m., so volunteers can also enjoy a full evening at home. Volunteers or your agency can provide food and beverages at the meetings and the meeting area should be comfortable.

PLAN YOUR MEETING

PLAN FOR WEEKLY VOLUNTEER SUPPORT MEETING

After you review the following sample agenda, create an agenda for your first meeting.

Sample Agenda

5:00–5:15	Volunteer sharing and brainstorming
5:15–5:20	Weekly agency announcements
5:20–5:50	Interpersonal communications workshop
5:50–6:00	Weekly volunteer recognition program

Your Agenda

_____

_____

_____

List five areas of major concern to your volunteers?

1. _____

2. _____

3. _____

4. _____

5. _____

How will you integrate these concerns into your weekly agenda?

_____

_____

What four skills would the volunteers like to develop?

1. _____ 2. _____

3. _____ 4. _____

How will you weave these skills into your agenda?

_____

_____

VOLUNTEER ASSIGNMENTS

As he or she becomes familiar with your agency's programs, it is common for a volunteer to request more or different responsibilities. How you adjust and modify his or her assignment can greatly enhance his or her contribution and value to your agency.

As you read the following volunteer case histories, decide how you would adjust each volunteer's assignment to meet his or her needs as well as your agency's needs:

CASE STUDY 1: Darwin, The Software Engineer

Darwin was working on the agency's annual fund-raising campaign. As his campaign responsibilities decreased, he discovered that the agency could use his technical expertise in developing a new computer database.

1. How should the agency adjust Darwin's fund-raising job, considering its programming needs?

_____

_____

_____

_____

2. How can the agency support Darwin with both of his agency responsibilities?

_____

_____

_____

_____

3. If Darwin's time becomes limited, how can the agency utilize Darwin's talents?

_____

_____

_____

_____

VOLUNTEER ASSIGNMENTS (continued)

CASE STUDY 2: Laura, The Public Relations Specialist

For the last three years, Laura coordinated publicity for the annual school play. Although she still wants to make a contribution to the play, Laura has become tired and bored with her publicity responsibilities.

1. How can the school utilize Laura's publicity experience without burdening her with the responsibility?

_____

_____

_____

_____

2. How can the school effectively recruit a new publicity chairperson and include Laura in the transition?

_____

_____

_____

_____

3. What should the school do with Laura's volunteer commitment this year?

_____

_____

_____

_____

Volunteers are empowered when an agency adjusts volunteers' assignments flexibly to meet volunteers' changing needs and personal interests.

MOTIVATE AND INSPIRE VOLUNTEERS

Motivated and inspired volunteers energize an agency. Volunteers are inspired to change their world when they are treated as professionals, flexibly and respectfully. Review the following motivational volunteer strategies:

1. Volunteer recognition programs can include ceremonial presentations with certificates, pins, gifts and privileges. Recognition is key to creating an overachiever, and it is the most effective strategy for developing motivation.

2. Standard forms of recognition include monthly evaluation and daily acknowledgement for positive performance.

3. Instant recognition strategies include ringing a bell for completion of projects and incentive contest winners.

4. Incentive programs motivate or acknowledge the accomplishment of a task, job or goal in a timely and efficient manner. The best incentives are those of long-term value or those that can be used daily. Incentives include trips, free meals, electronic components and special privileges.

5. Sprints and instant daily recognition include candy, wine, groceries and money.

AGENCY PLAN FOR RECOGNITION

How does your agency acknowledge its volunteers' contributions?

_____

_____

_____

_____

How often does your agency formally recognize volunteers?

_____

_____

_____

_____

What types of recognitions and incentives have your volunteers received?

_____

_____

_____

_____

What can you do to increase your volunteers' motivation and inspiration?

_____

_____

_____

_____

What volunteer recognition privileges can your agency provide?

_____

_____

_____

_____

PERIODIC VOLUNTEER CAREER ASSESSMENT

As volunteers develop new skills through their agency experiences, some will consider changing careers. How you relate to these volunteers is critical for their career assessment and growth. Consider the following case histories and answer the questions at the end of each case:

CASE HISTORY 1 Amanda, The Former Production Worker

Amanda felt fulfilled after she started working with children at her daughter's nursery school. In addition, Amanda spent hours reading child development books so her daughter would have the childhood she never experienced.

After a forced layoff, Amanda reconsidered her career and then approached the nursery school director about her interest. After several discussions, Amanda registered in a child development program at the local junior college. Within a short period of time, she completed the preliminary child care classes. With a child care permit, she was able to work at a nursery school while continuing her education.

1. When first approached, what do you think the nursery school director said to Amanda, which motivated her to approach the college?

   _____

   _____

   _____

2. What questions do you think the director asked Amanda about her interest in child development?

   _____

   _____

   _____

3. What could the director have done to help Amanda in her college assessment and training?

   _____

   _____

   _____

PERIODIC VOLUNTEER CAREER ASSESSMENT (continued)

CASE STUDY 2: Frank, The Former Insurance Agent

Following high school, Frank decided to sell life insurance. After a lot of cold prospecting and sales, he established his own business. As part of his commitment to his community, Frank served on the board of a local nonprofit organization. After several experiences with nonprofit legal issues, Frank realized he was interested in becoming a public administrator.

Once he made that decision, he approached the agency's executive director about his career plan. Through her expert guidance, within a few months he was admitted into a local program.

1. As the agency's executive director, what would be your initial reaction to Frank's interest?

   _____

   _____

   _____

2. How would you help Frank identify appropriate community resources and educational experiences?

   _____

   _____

   _____

3. What resources would you provide Frank after he enters the college program?

   _____

   _____

   _____

VOLUNTEER EMPOWERMENT WITHIN YOUR ORGANIZATION

Organizational empowerment occurs when the agency enables its volunteers and staff to do all they can for the betterment of the organization. Volunteers are empowered when they believe:

- They can contribute all of their talents to the agency

- There are no set rules or requirements within the agency

- Agency staff will take the time to listen to new ideas

- The agency respects and trusts its volunteers

- The agency will provide support and resources

Empowered volunteers have positive attitudes about their potential and roles in an agency. Following are three positive attitude examples:

Example 1:

Theresa was upset when she was told that the paper she had written did not fulfill specific project requirements. At first she felt that she had wasted her time and was disappointed with her performance. She reconsidered when she realized that writing the paper a second time would strengthen her writing skills.

Example 2:

Bob was exasperated when he learned he had to drive across town to pick up a document in commute traffic. Once he was in the car, he decided to make the most of the opportunity. He mentally worked through a project report due the next day and discovered that the change in scenery and activity stimulated his creativity.

Example 3:

As a publicity agency volunteer, Rita was frustrated that the agency did not have a consistent list of publicity contacts. After researching the needs of the agency, Rita designed a media and community services database.

IS YOUR AGENCY RESPONSIVE?

Once volunteers feel positive about their potential within the agency, it is critical that the agency continually encourage them to make recommendations for change.

Consider the following questions, and evaluate how your agency would respond:

1. Does your agency consider all of a volunteer's knowledge and experiences when assigning him or her to a job?

_____

_____

_____

2. How accepting and flexible is your agency to new ideas?

_____

_____

_____

3. How often do you make yourself available to volunteers?

_____

_____

_____

4. Do you treat your volunteers as part of the team or as a separate entity?

_____

_____

_____

5. How do you support your volunteers?

_____

_____

_____

ONGOING EVALUATION AND ADJUSTMENT

As your agency responds to the creative energies of your volunteers, ongoing agency evaluation and adjustments are essential. Your volunteers are your agency's bloodline to the community. Their nurturing and maturation are essential to your agency's health and development. This, or a similar form, should be a part of your agency's regularly scheduled, ongoing evaluation process:

Agency Evaluation Form

Circle the appropriate numerical value for each item.

	Low				High
1. Valuing of volunteers in your agency	1	2	3	4	5
2. Visualizing your agency's future	1	2	3	4	5
3. Understanding the purpose of each agency function	1	2	3	4	5
4. Understanding the skills for each functional role	1	2	3	4	5
5. Utilizing agency volunteers	1	2	3	4	5
6. Volunteer recruitment strategies	1	2	3	4	5
7. Volunteer evaluation and role assignments	1	2	3	4	5
8. Volunteer training	1	2	3	4	5
9. Volunteer support	1	2	3	4	5
10. Volunteer empowerment	1	2	3	4	5

Review your answers. Which areas in your agency's volunteer recruitment and development does your agency need to further develop?

_____

_____

What is your plan for action?

_____

_____

INDEX OF FORMS

NOTES

FOR OTHER FIFTY-MINUTE SELF-STUDY BOOKS
SEE THE BACK OF THIS BOOK.

$$\boxed{\textbf{NOTES}}$$

FOR OTHER FIFTY-MINUTE SELF-STUDY BOOKS
SEE THE BACK OF THIS BOOK.

ABOUT THE FIFTY-MINUTE SERIES

We hope you enjoyed this book and found it valuable. If so, we have good news for you. This title is part of the best selling *FIFTY-MINUTE Series* of books. All *Series* books are similar in size and format, and identical in price. Several are supported with training videos. These are identified by the symbol **V** next to the title.

Since the first *FIFTY-MINUTE* book appeared in 1986, millions of copies have been sold worldwide. Each book was developed with the reader in mind. The result is a concise, high quality module written in a positive, readable self-study format.

FIFTY-MINUTE Books and Videos are available from your distributor. A free current catalog is available on request from Crisp Publications, Inc., 95 First Street, Los Altos, CA 94022.

Following is a complete list of *FIFTY-MINUTE Series* Books and Videos organized by general subject area.

Management Training (continued):

Personal Improvement:

Human Resources & Wellness:

Small Business & Financial Planning:

Adult Literacy & Learning:

Career/Retirement & Life Planning: